Books should be returned on or before the
last date stamped below

ANNE FRANK

Emma Johnson

FRANKLIN WATTS
LONDON•SYDNEY

Editor-in-Chief John C. Miles
Picture Research Susan Mennell

Consultant Eileen Yeo
Professor of Social and Cultural
History, University of Strathclyde

© 2002 Franklin Watts

First published in 2002
by Franklin Watts
96 Leonard Street
London
EC2A 4XD

Franklin Watts Australia
56 O'Riordan Street
Alexandria
NSW 2015

ISBN 0 7496 4648 9

Dewey classification: 940.53

A CIP catalogue record
for this book is available
from the British Library.

Printed in Hong Kong/China

Picture credits
Front and back cover images: AKG
London
©AFF/AFS, Amsterdam, the
Netherlands pp.43, 48, 51, 64, 72
AKG London pp.2,3,5,9,10,12-13, 15,
16-17, 20, 21, 23, 25, 26-27, 28, 30-
31, 32-33, 39, 40 (right), 44-45, 60,
63, 71, 76-77, 78, 81, 83, 84-85, 88,
93, 95, 96
Hulton Archive pp.6, 55, 100,
Topham Picturepoint pp.36-37, 40
(left and background), 53, 56, 58-59,
68-69, 90, 99, 101, 102-103

Text credits
Quotes from
THE DIARY OF A YOUNG GIRL: THE
DEFINITIVE EDITION by Anne Frank,
edited by Otto H Frank and Mirjam
Pressler, translated by Susan Massotty
(Viking, 1997), copyright © The Anne
Frank-Fonds, Basle,Switzerland, 1991.

THE DIARY OF A YOUNG GIRL: THE
DEFINITIVE EDITION by Anne Frank.
Otto H Frank & Mirjam Pressler,
Editors, translated by Susan Massotty,
copyright © 1995 by Doubleday, a
division of Random House, Inc. Used
by permission of Doubleday, a division
of Random House, Inc.

Anne Frank
1929-1945

Contents

Introduction

Anne Frank, a young Jewish girl, was born in Germany in 1929. She experienced the growth of anti-Semitism during the 1930s. Fleeing with her family to apparent safety in the Netherlands, she was later caught up in the terrible persecution of the Jews by the Nazis in World War Two.

Anne's diary gives us an insight into what it was like to be Jewish in Europe at the time of the Second World War. By the end of that war, at least six million Jews had been killed. To understand how this could have happened, it is important to know how life changed in Germany after 1918.

Millions of soldiers worldwide were killed during World War One (1914–18). For Germans, the war was even more disastrous – after their country's defeat it had to pay huge reparations (sums of money) to its allied opponents – France, Britain and America. In addition, Germany's head of state, Kaiser Wilhelm II, went into exile in Belgium in 1918, where he lived until his death in 1941.

These events destabilized Germany, both economically and politically. Out of this instability a dictator in the person of Adolf Hitler emerged. As he rose to power Hitler manipulated public opinion. First he obtained power by democratic means; later he ruthlessly crushed democracy to ensure his own power as the leader of a new "German Empire".

Germany and World War One

By the end of the 19th century, Germany had become one of the strongest military and industrial powers in the world. The increased might and ambition of Germany threatened the older European countries (France, Russia and Great Britain). Growing tension came to a head when Archduke Franz Ferdinand, heir to the throne of Austria-Hungary, was assassinated in 1914. Russia jumped to the defence of Serbia, who were accused of sponsoring the killing, while Germany did the same for Austria-Hungary. Soon, other world powers were brought into the conflict. The war lasted for four years, ending with Germany's defeat in 1918.

Growing up in Frankfurt

Anne Frank was born on 12 June 1929 in the prosperous German city of Frankfurt am Main. Her full given name was Annelies Marie Frank.

At the time Frankfurt was an important commercial centre with a history dating back to medieval times. The city had always boasted a large Jewish population and in the year of Anne's birth, there were about 30,000 Jews out of a total population of 540,000.

The "new liberalism"

At the beginning of the 19th century Frankfurt's Jewish ghetto, the *Judengasse*, had been demolished and laws were passed to give equal rights to the Jewish population. Jews were free to integrate or live a traditional way of life as they chose. A symbol of this "new liberalism" was the building of the Borneplatz Synagogue in 1882, in a thriving, popular section next to the huge open-air market. By the end

▶ *Margot (left) and Anne with their father Otto in 1930. Anne was one year old.*

Otto's war service for Germany

Otto, together with his brothers Robert and Herbert, were among the estimated 100,000 German Jews who fought for Germany in World War One. As a lieutenant, Otto Frank outranked Corporal Hitler. Had the two men been members of the same unit, Hitler would have been in the position of having to take orders from Otto.

of the 19th century new industrial areas had grown on the east and west side of the city. By 1918 Frankfurt had overrun its neighbouring villages to become the largest German city in land area.

Otto and Edith Frank

Anne's father, Otto, was born in the affluent Westend area of the city in 1889. His parents belonged to the Liberal Jewish congregation and had friends of different faiths and backgrounds. Although anti-Semitism had been rife in Frankfurt for centuries, Otto later claimed that he never encountered an anti-Semite in his youth in Frankfurt. At the age of 19, after finishing high school and studying art history at Heidelberg University for just one term, Otto was offered work in Macy's department store in New York City. He jumped at the chance to travel and soon grew to love New York. However, after the death of his father, he returned to Germany in 1909. Back home, he found work with an engineering company in Düsseldorf, until the outbreak of World War One in 1914.

Anne's mother, Edith Holländer was born and grew up in Aachen, close to the Belgian and Dutch border, where her father worked in manufacturing. Otto and Edith met through the Franks' business and were married in 1925. Otto was 36 and Edith was 25. Although they were not madly in love, they had much in common. On 16 February, 1926, Anne's elder sister Margot Betti Frank was born.

The Jewish ghettos

Many Jews had settled in Germany in the Middle Ages, seeking refuge from persecution in other parts of Europe. The Jewish Ghetto, which had its beginnings in 16th-century Italy, was an isolated area of town set aside for the Jewish community. Pope Paul IV granted the Jews protection from persecution on the understanding that they paid taxes. Many ghettos were thriving places, where the skills of Jewish merchants and tradesmen added to the overall prosperity of the town.

By June 1929, the month in which Anne was born, Otto was well established, working for his father's bank in Frankfurt. Anne's family belonged to the wealthy middle classes, which had solid roots in Germany and had fought for their country in World War One.

In the early part of the twentieth century, Frankfurt was a reasonably tolerant place, but throughout the 1920s there was frequent unrest and the large Jewish population often found themselves under threat of attack from the National Socialists (the Nazis), an extreme, nationalistic political party that blamed Jews and Communists for Germany's defeat in World War One. Despite this strand of anti-Semitism, business was good and life was comfortable for the Frank family.

Anne's early years

The first years of Anne's life were spent in happy circumstances. In 1931 the family moved to 24 Ganghoferstrasse, an up-and-coming neighbourhood known as the Poets' Quarter. Otto Frank, a keen amateur photographer, took numerous photographs of Anne and Margot playing at home and with friends, and on family holidays and outings. An early photo of Anne shows her in hospital, a one-day-old baby in her mother's arms. Other photos record the loving relationship between the sisters in early childhood, time spent with their grandparents, and visits from their close cousins, Stephan and Buddy. As they grew up, the girls' individual characters emerged: Margot was kind-hearted and shy and looked very much like her mother; Anne was lively, funny, and outgoing, more like her father. As the slightly spoilt younger daughter, she was her "daddy's girl". Both girls adored their father, who often told them bedtime stories about two girls named Paula, one good and one mischievous.

Economic slump

On 24 October 1929 (a day later referred to as Black Thursday), America's stock market collapsed. The "Wall Street Crash" ushered in an economic slump, a period known as the Great Depression, which lasted until the beginning of the Second World War in 1939. For Germany, still paying huge debts from the 1914–18 war, this was a disaster. The government (the National Assembly) began to lose control, leaving only the German Labour

Movement and various left-wing groups to oppose Adolf Hitler's popular right-wing Nazi Party, who promised a great German revival.

In the year of Anne's birth, German banknotes became practically worthless and in Frankfurt, by the end of 1932, more than 70,000 workers were unemployed. Trade union membership in Germany reached 12 million; the unions began to demand that the government introduce rationing of essentials to help control the economic crisis. The situation became so bad that the desperate German people began to look to extremists for solutions to their problems. As a result, the Nazi Party began to recruit more and more followers. At first, Hitler blamed

▼ *Throughout the 1920s, as the economic situation in Germany worsened, the dole queues grew longer.*

Propaganda and "spin"

The Nazis were the first political party to use propaganda to manipulate the public and justify their actions. Putting a "spin" on real facts and statistics to encourage people to agree with your point of view is not uncommon in politics today. This manipulation of the truth was so important to the Nazis that they formulated very disciplined methods of communicating with the public, through printed material (like this romanticized illustration of Hitler), radio broadcasts and mass rallies.

the government for being weak. Later, he accused the Jews of not only causing but also exploiting the terrible German economic situation to their advantage, at the expense of "honest German people". Hitler's selection of the Jews as scapegoats happened at a time when many people were looking for someone to blame for their misfortune. His twisted views, expressed in his book *Mein Kampf* (*My Struggle*), together with his political ambitions, proved to be horribly effective. As his party gathered support, Jews found that their position within German society was becoming untenable.

In the September 1930 elections Hitler's Nazi Party became the second-largest party. The number of people who had voted for the Nazis had increased from 800,000 in 1928 to nearly 6.5 million. On 11 October 1931 Germany's right-wing political parties joined together to demand new elections. The following year, general elections were held and Hitler won 37 per cent of the 13.5 million vote. At first he headed a coalition government, but later he

◄ *Adolf Hitler's Nazi party rose to prominence with promises to make Germany great again. This poster portrays Hitler as the leader of the German people.*

Nazi thug tactics

Nazis did not just use "spin" and propaganda to gain power. They also used brute force. In 1921 Hitler had founded the SA division of the Nazi party, also known as the Storm Troopers or Brownshirts. They were his assault troops, made up mainly of ex-soldiers and other militant, rough characters. The SA carried out street assaults on German Jews and Nazi opponents, and intimidated voters during elections. The SA played a key role in Hitler's rise to power.

exploited the divided opposition to become Chancellor (Prime Minister) of Germany in January 1933.

In Frankfurt, two months later, the Nazi Party received a large share of the council votes. Nazi supporters gathered outside the town hall, raising their hands in the Nazi salute as they shouted, "Heil Hitler! Down with the Jews!". The same month saw hundreds arrested as the Nazis rounded up their political opponents and stepped up their repression of the Jews.

When the Franks lived there, Frankfurt was a bustling cosmopolitan city. This is a view from the mid-1930s.

From Germany to Holland

On 5 March 1933 the German people voted again. This time, the Nazi party won 44 per cent of the vote and on 23 March the Enabling Law was passed.

This new law allowed Hitler to ignore the constitution and ratify any law he cared to make. On 14 July all other political parties were declared illegal – Hitler's power was absolute. Served by a close circle of associates, which included Joseph Goebbels, Hermann Goering, Heinrich Himmler and Reinhard Heydrich, he declared Germany to be the Third Reich (Empire).

Hitler crushes opposition

Hitler's first political acts removed or suppressed any opposition. The German Labour movement was one of his first targets. During March 1933, 10,000 active trade union members were arrested and in May of that year the leaders of the unions were replaced by Nazi Party members. All workers were now forced to join the DAF (German Workers Front), which was controlled by the Nazis. Employers and their workers were forced to co-operate with Hitler's government; strikes were not tolerated. At Oranienburg, near Berlin, a "concentration camp" was built to hold opponents to the Nazi regime. In 1933 150,000 people were sent there for so-called "re-education".

German churches soon endorsed the Nazis' political and racial policies. There were a few exceptions, but on 28 March 1933, Catholic bishops lifted their ban on parishioners becoming members of the Nazi Party. Persecution of the Jews and other minorities went on without a word of protest from the official churches. Only the Bekennende church,

▶ *The Nazis relied on elaborate rallies to maintain power by fear, as here at Nuremburg in 1938 .*

a Protestant group, objected to the outrageous injustices from the outset.

Isolating Jewish people

In Frankfurt, the Jewish mayor was replaced by a Nazi, and a swastika flag – the official Nazi symbol – was raised above the city's town hall. In April 1933 Joseph Goebbels, now Minister for Propaganda, declared an official boycott of all Jewish teachers, doctors, lawyers and shopkeepers. Later that month all civil servants with Jewish ancestry were fired from their jobs. Apart from these official acts, dozens of obstructive measures were used to make sure that life quickly became impossible for the majority of Jews in Germany. Nazi philosophy stated that there was only room in the country for Aryan (pure-bred white) Germans. Jewish business owners were forced to sell to their Aryan countrymen at knockdown prices and to witness the dismissal of any Jewish staff.

It was most likely during the first months of 1933 that Otto Frank began to consider leaving his country. When Hitler became Chancellor of Germany,

◄ *Another Nuremburg rally, this time of the Nazi Party's youth wing, or "Hitler Youth", in 1933.*

17

there were about 500,000 Jews living in the cities and throughout the countryside. As the various decrees against them mounted, increasingly isolating them from the rest of the population, many Jews who could afford to leave Germany did so.

Most fled with nothing, taking up work in the clothing or diamond industries in other European countries, America or Britain. Otto's sister Leni and her husband Erich, together with their children Stephan and Buddy, left in 1933. The same year Otto's mother went to Basel, Switzerland to join her daughter. By now Jews were not recognized as German citizens and their children were excluded from schools attended by non-Jews. This meant that Anne was unable to go to the nursery of her parents' choice and Margot had to leave the school she loved. Otto and Edith were only too aware of the worsening situation.

The move to Amsterdam

There were several reasons why Otto Frank chose to take his family to Holland. He had friends there, it was familiar and, perhaps more importantly, Dutch policy on refugees was more liberal than in most other countries. In World War One, Holland and Switzerland had been neutral. Both countries expected to remain neutral even if a new war broke out. So, when his brother-in-law arranged for him to work in the Dutch office of his company in Amsterdam, Otto grabbed the opportunity to get his family out of Germany. In 1933, as the Nazi Party gathered support, the Franks were among 63,000 Jews to leave. Anne and Margot stayed with their grandmother in Aachen until their parents were settled. Margot joined her parents in Amsterdam in December 1933 and Anne followed in February 1934. Early on in her diary Anne explained that when she arrived in Amsterdam, "I was plonked down on the table as a birthday present for Margot."

In Amsterdam, Otto soon became Managing Director of the Opekta Company, which manufactured spices and pectin, used in jam-making. The family moved into a house on Merwedeplein in Amsterdam's River Quarter and Anne and Margot attended the local Montessori school. They made friends both at school and with other Jewish immigrant families living nearby.

Fascism appears in Holland

Even in Holland, traditionally a liberal nation, the fascist movement had gained a foothold. In 1931 Anton Mussert founded the National Socialist Movement (NSB), which was modelled on the German Nazi Party. Many people who had no faith in the main political parties in the Netherlands joined this new right-wing group. A year after Anne arrived in Amsterdam, a general election was held and the National Socialist Movement obtained 8 per cent of the votes cast. Otto and Edith Frank must have been relieved when, in 1936, the NSB's popularity started to wane. This was due to its anti-Semitism and the fact that its leadership did not have the ruthlessness of its German counterpart.

Events back in Germany

The years between 1934 and 1940 were secure and happy for the Franks in the Netherlands. However, in Germany, the Nazis were consolidating their hold. Anne's parents were determined to keep news of the worsening situation from their children for as long as possible.

During the 1930s, further laws were introduced to authorize the forced sterilization of any individual deemed likely to produce "genetically unfit" offspring. Laws forbidding marriage between Jews and non-Jews were passed in 1935, and in 1937 Hitler's secret state police, the *Gestapo*, took nearly 400 black and mixed-race German children to hospital for sterilization. In 1939 Anne's maternal grandmother moved from Aachen to join the family in Amsterdam.

German laws to isolate Jews

By 1938 Jews had no legal rights at all. Hitler showed how simple it was to isolate a people in their own country.
- German children were forbidden to speak to Jews
- Jews who had passports were ordered to hand them in
- Jewish property was confiscated and businesses closed down
- Jews were forbidden to deal in property, jewellery or precious metals or freely operate bank accounts
- In Munich, Jews were given 48 hours to leave or else go to concentration camps

The "Night of broken glass"

On 9–10 November, 1938 the event that became known as "*Kristallnacht*" or "Night of broken glass" took place. Dozens of synagogues, including Frankfurt's

▶ *A woman surveys damage to a Jewish shop in Berlin as a result of Kristallnacht, 9-10 November 1938.*

▲ *Kristallnacht damage was not confined to Jewish businesses. This is the interior of the Okel Jaakov synagogue in Munich on 10 November 1938.*

Borneplatz, and thousands of Jewish shops in Germany and Austria were broken into and set on fire. During this night of outrage, which left shattered glass on the streets, German men and women were seen jeering at Jews and encouraging their attackers.

Then on 12 November, around 30,000 Jewish men and boys were arrested and taken to Dachau, Buchenwald and Sachsenhausen concentration camps. This was the first deadly step on the path towards what the Nazis were to call "The Final Solution".

Invasion of Holland

Adolf Hitler secured the support of the German armed forces early on in his "reign of terror". He pandered to their sense of pride, reminding them about the loss of German territory after World War One and the need to erase the shame of their country's defeat.

Hitler planned to regain former German territories and expand the German border east to gain new "living space" (referred to as *Lebensraum*). The military agreed to support him only if he limited the brutal power of the two and a half million-strong SA or Brownshirts. On 30 June 1934 the SA leaders were murdered on Hitler's orders and at the end of the same year the German army swore allegiance directly to Hitler.

Germany begins invasions

Rearmament started in 1934, and by the middle of 1935 military conscription was reintroduced. In 1938, the German army invaded Czechoslovakia and the old German territory of the Sudetenland. Hitler's next target was Poland and despite Britain's threat to go to war with Germany if Hitler invaded, the Germans crossed into Polish territory in September 1939. This invasion was the spark that ignited World War Two.

The Maginot Line

As in World War One, France and Britain were allied against Germany. Since 1918 the French had built an enormous fortified line with massive gun emplacements, subterranean armouries and barracks for the troops who manned it. Known as the Maginot Line, it was believed to be proof against any German attack. The northern end of the Maginot Line terminated at the Belgian border.

▶ *A view of Amsterdam in the 1930s.*

For the first nine months after war was declared, an uneasy silence settled across Europe – this period was known as the "Phoney War". By 1940 Holland had absorbed about 24,000 Jewish refugees, swelling the total population of Jews living there to 140,000, of which 90,000 were living in Amsterdam. This city now held the largest Jewish population in Europe.

On 10 May 1940 the Germans surprised everyone by launching an attack on the Netherlands. Dutch neutrality had been violated and the Maginot Line rendered useless as a defence for France. The Germans dropped paratroopers and quickly seized all the key areas of the country within a few days. Brisk fighting forced the Dutch government and royal family to flee to Britain. On 15 May 1940, Holland capitulated. This followed the bombing of Rotterdam, during which more than 900 people were killed and 24,000 houses destroyed. The country was now under German occupation.

"Blitzkrieg"

Throughout the summer months of 1940 the German occupying forces in Holland were careful not to antagonize the Dutch people. This was because the German army was engaged in its "Blitzkrieg" campaign across Belgium and northern France. When the French army realized that the Maginot Line provided no defence and French troops were cut off by the Germans' rapid advance, they gave up. The British had been forced to retreat to the French coast, where an extraordinary rescue took place at Dunkirk. An armada of small civilian boats turned up and took the troops off the beaches and safely back to England.

The display of German military supremacy heralded new laws in the Netherlands. These included the imposition of the black-out, issuing of ration cards and, in May 1941, compulsory carrying of identity cards.

In the autumn of 1940 the Nazis took the first step towards persecution of the Jews in Holland. A "Declaration of Aryanism" form was presented to civil servants, judges, employers and teachers asking if any of their parents or grandparents were Jewish. Almost the entire population of the country filled in these forms, and the information provided made the next stages of the Jewish persecution easy.

▲ *German aircraft, loaded with paratroops, launch the first wave of the assault on Holland on 10 May 1940.*

Persecuting Jews in Holland

As in Germany, between 1933 and 1938, anti-Jewish measures were taken in Holland increasingly to isolate Jews.

In February 1941 Mussert's paramilitary arm of the NSB, the Weer-Afdeling, entered Amsterdam's Jewish quarter, deliberately provoking trouble by raiding the markets on Amstelveld and Waterloo Square. Heavy fighting followed when

▼ *A column of German cavalry advances through a Dutch village in 1940.*

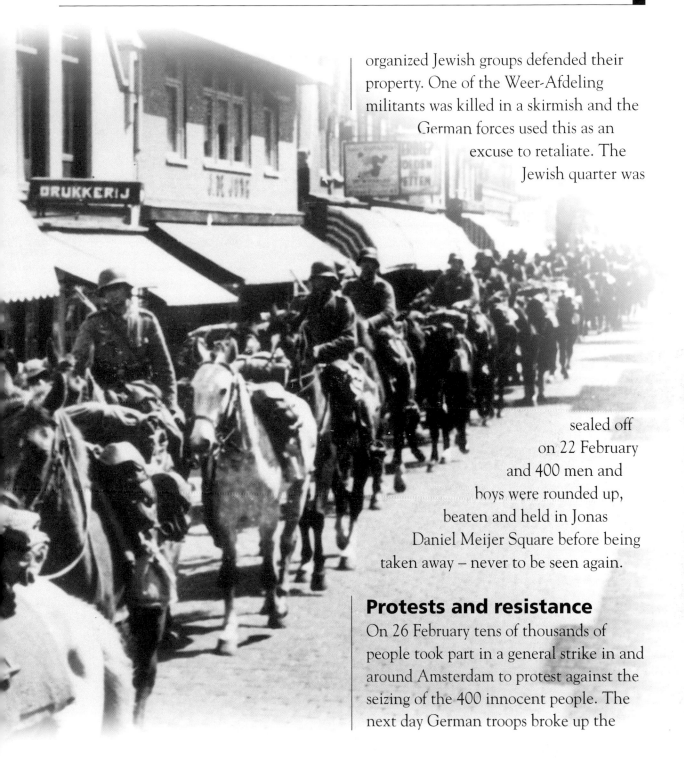

organized Jewish groups defended their property. One of the Weer-Afdeling militants was killed in a skirmish and the German forces used this as an excuse to retaliate. The Jewish quarter was

sealed off on 22 February and 400 men and boys were rounded up, beaten and held in Jonas Daniel Meijer Square before being taken away – never to be seen again.

Protests and resistance

On 26 February tens of thousands of people took part in a general strike in and around Amsterdam to protest against the seizing of the 400 innocent people. The next day German troops broke up the

strike, firing live rounds of ammunition and arresting people indiscriminately. The strike ended when the people realized the Nazis had no qualms about further reprisals if the strike continued. Several months later death notices reached relatives of those taken in the February round-up, stating that the arrested men and boys had been killed in Mauthausen concentration camp.

Although the majority of the Dutch population were anti-Nazi, a large minority collaborated with the Germans. These were members of the various national socialist organizations, such as Mussert's NSB. The Dutch Union (NU) was founded to provide a focus of protest against German Nazism, but it also looked for ways to co-operate with the German authorities so that it could maintain its independence. In 1941, following its protest against anti-Jewish laws, the NU was banned. The Union had learned, to its cost, that the Nazis were not interested in compromise.

By 1942 most of the anti-Jewish decrees were in place. Anne listed them

◄ The Nazis forced Dutch Jews – such as these people in Amsterdam – to wear a yellow star with the word Jood (Jew) on it.

in her diary entry for 20 June 1942. They match those in place in Germany in the years between 1933 and 1938. Jews were required to wear a yellow cloth star with the word Jood on their clothes. They had to hand in their bicycles to the authorities and were forbidden to use trams or ride in cars, even if the car was their own. Jewish children were banned from state schools and were forced to attend special Jewish ones. Jews had to do their shopping between 3.00 and 5.00 p.m., and were required to go to Jewish-owned barbers and beauty salons. They were forbidden to go to theatres, cinemas or other forms of entertainment and were banned from using sporting facilities or taking part in any athletic activity in public. Jews had to observe a curfew and were not allowed out on the streets or even into their own gardens after 8.00 p.m. They were forbidden to visit Christians in their homes. These restrictions were designed to segregate the Jews from the rest of Dutch society. But they also fanned anti-Semitic feeling, encouraging Dutch Christians to regard Jews as outsiders who posed a dangerous threat to the so-called "Dutch Aryan" way of life.

The diary

Soon after arriving in Holland, Anne began her schooling. In the spring of 1934 she started at a Montessori nursery school, which was close to the Franks' house on Merwedeplein.

Anne was a promising pupil and at the age of seven was already reading and writing well. If Anne seemed to be a good student, her elder sister Margot was definitely the scholar of the family. Anne later recorded in her diary: "Margot has also got her report. Brilliant as usual. If we had such a thing as 'cum laude', she would have passed with honours."

At the Montessori school Anne had both Jewish and Christian friends. She was attractive and popular, regarding herself as a bit of a clown. Among her early close friends were Sanne Ledermann and Hanneli Goslar. As a trio, the girls were known as "Anne, Hanne and Sanne". Hanneli (Lies) later recalled how Anne would entertain her classmates and make them laugh. She could dislocate her shoulder at will, a trick she enjoyed

▶ *The Nazis wasted no time in strengthening their grip on Holland. This picture shows the Reichskommisar (governor) of the Netherlands, Arthur Seyss-Inquart, watching a parade of Nazi military police in Amsterdam on 10 February 1941.*

performing to an appreciative audience. Lies also acknowledged Anne's early literary promise, saying that her writing was "very mature" for her age.

In the summer of 1941, as a result of German orders demanding segregation of Christians and Jews in Holland, Anne was accepted at the Jewish Lyceum, which her sister Margot was attending. Anne recorded her emotional farewell to Mrs Kuperus, the headmistress of her first school – "we were both in tears as we said a heartbreaking farewell". At the lyceum Anne met Jacqueline van Maarsen and they soon became best friends, collecting and swapping postcards of film stars. In the summer of 1941, Edith's mother, the girls' dear Granny, became seriously ill and had to have an operation. She had lived with the family since 1939, when she had been persuaded to leave Germany for good. When she died in the winter of 1941-42, Anne wrote: "No one will ever know how much she is in my thoughts and how much I love her still."

◀ *Otto and Anne (second row, left-hand page) walk with other guests to a wedding on 16 July 1941. Anne's mother Edith stayed at home with Margot, who was ill.*

Anne receives the diary

At 6.00 a.m. on Friday, 12 June 1942, Anne woke up, full of excitement – it was her 13th birthday. She wasn't usually encouraged to get up so early, so she forced herself to stay in bed for another 45 minutes. At a quarter to seven she went into the family's dining room and played with Moortje, their cat. Then, unable to wait any longer, she went to find her parents and with them went to the living room to open her presents. Among the gifts was a red and white cloth-covered diary with a simple lock on the front, from her father. Anne was thrilled. Her first entry reads: "I hope I will be able to confide everything to you, as I have never been able to confide in anyone, and hope you will be a great source of comfort and support."

"Dearest Kitty"

Anne decided to personalize her diary as if she were confiding in her closest friend. She called the diary "Kitty" (after a character in a novel she liked) and usually started each entry with "Dearest Kitty". She stuck a photograph of herself on the inside cover and wrote: "Gorgeous photograph, isn't it!!!!"

Early diary entries were concerned with recording the events of her birthday and describing her school friends, their personalities and how they behaved. Like many girls of her age, she was very interested in boys. Hanneli (Lies) Goslar recalled: "Boys really liked her and she always liked it a lot when all the boys paid attention to her." Anne documented her opinions of all the boys in her class. She was a harsh critic, using descriptions such as "brat", "pest" and "obnoxious, two-faced, lying, snivelling little twit". Only one boy escaped unscathed. Anne said: "Harry Schap is the most decent boy in the class."

Hobbies and interests

Describing her hobbies and interests to "Kitty", "to lay the basis for our friendship", she wrote about the table tennis club she founded with four other girls. They called it "The Little Dipper, Minus Two", because they wanted a special name and thought the Little Dipper was made up of five stars. Later they discovered there were seven stars in this constellation, so they added the "Minus Two". The girls liked ice-cream, so after their matches they would cycle to the nearest ice-cream parlour that was allowed to serve Jews. They usually found boys who would buy them "more ice-cream than we could eat in a week".

In her diary Anne described her encounters with boys who wanted to cycle home with her and "were sure to fall for me on the spot". Often she would think up ruses to put the boys off. These included distraction and pretence. She might swerve her bike and let her satchel fall to the ground. While the boy stopped to pick it up, Anne had time to think of a way to steer the conversation. At other times, she would pretend to be insulted at something the boy said or did and insist that he went home without her.

"An incorrigible chatterbox"

Anne got on quite well with her teachers at the Jewish school. Mr Keesing, who taught maths, complained that she talked too much in class. After several warnings, he gave her some extra homework – to write an essay on being "A Chatterbox". Anne wrote three pages, arguing that talking is a female trait and that since her mother talked as much as she did, she had inherited this fault. She would do her best to control it, but might never be able "to cure herself of the habit".

Mr Keesing had a tough job with Anne; no sooner was the essay handed in than Anne was chattering in class again. He set her another essay, the title of which was to be "An Incorrigible Chatterbox". After this Anne managed to be quiet for two whole lessons, but returned to chatting during the third. Finally, Keesing set her an essay entitled "Quack, Quack, said Mistress Chatterback". The whole class erupted in laughter as Anne was set the challenge of producing something original. Anne's friend Sanne, who was a budding poet, offered to help her write it in verse. Anne jumped at the chance of producing a clever piece of work and the poem was a great success when read aloud.

A few days after this classroom incident, Anne met a 16 year-old boy called Hello (Helmuth) Silberberg at a friend's house. He liked Anne and was soon cycling to school with her. Anne was flattered by his attentions, although she claimed to be in love with a boy called Peter Schiff, whom she had not seen for some time. When she saw Peter in the street while out with Helmuth, and he said hello to her, "it really made me feel good", she wrote. One evening Hello came over to Anne's house to visit. After a while they went for a walk and didn't get back to the Franks' house until ten minutes after the curfew time of 8.00 p.m. Anne's father was waiting anxiously for her return. He scolded her for her thoughtlessness and made her promise that in future she would be home before the curfew time, at ten minutes to eight. Later, Anne's mother teased her by asking whom she was going to marry. Anne's response was typically cheeky: "I bet she'll never guess it's Peter, because I talked her out of that idea myself."

A young girl's scrapbook

Anne stuck family snapshots into her diary, together with comments. Whenever she wanted to add anything, she would stick some loose sheets of paper inside. She also used two types of handwriting in the diary; printing and joined up writing. On 20 June 1942 she wrote: "It's an odd idea for someone like me to keep a diary; not only because I have never done so before, but because it seems to me that neither I – nor for that matter anyone else – will be interested in the unbosomings of a thirteen-year-old schoolgirl."

▶ *Anne's diary, a precious gift on her thirteenth birthday, became her special confidante.*

Going into hiding

Throughout 1941 Otto Frank began making arrangements to take his family into hiding. Otto's business had changed premises on 1 December 1940, moving to 263 Prinsengracht. It was here that Otto prepared a secret annexe, on the top two floors at the rear of the building.

In January 1942 the first "call-up" papers were served to Jews in Holland. At first only unemployed Jewish males were called upon to report for work in the eastern Netherlands. But soon whole families were summoned to go to Westerbork camp, formerly a transit camp for Jewish refugees seeking entry into Holland. From there the families were sent east to labour camps in overcrowded cattle cars, which had no heating, toilets or seating. Prisoners were given no food or water. The Jewish Council was pressured by the Nazis to deliver specific numbers of people to the camp at Westerbork. The quota was not met, so arrests were made at random by the Nazi special police force – the dreaded SS. Many Jews tried to find hiding places, mostly in the countryside, but only a small number were successful.

Otto Frank's plan

Because of the way in which events had unfolded in Germany, Otto Frank had anticipated the Nazis' anti-Jewish actions in Holland. In 1941 he had transferred the ownership of his business to two of his senior employees – Johannes (Jo) Kleiman and Victor Kugler – and the business name was changed from "Opekta – Works" to "Trading Company Gies & Co". Kugler and Kleiman, as well as Miep Gies and Elisabeth "Bep" Voskuijl, Otto's female office staff, were to become the Frank family's lifeline for two years.

While out walking with Anne one day, Otto told her something of his plans to take the family into hiding. On the morning of 5 July 1942 Anne chronicled in her diary his concern about living "cut

▶ *The deportation of Jewish families usually began at a railway station.*

▲ Front and back views of the house at 263 Prinsengracht, Amsterdam, where Otto Frank's business was situated and where the Frank family would spend more than two years in hiding. The "Secret Annexe" is on the upper floors at the back.

off from the world" and her own anxiety about this unexpected turn of events. During the afternoon the front doorbell rang at their home. It was a hot summer's day and Anne was sunbathing and reading outside on the flat roof. She didn't hear the bell, but a little later, a shaken Margot came up and told her that their father had received a "call-up" notice from the SS. This meant that he would be sent to a concentration camp and probably to his death. Later Margot admitted to Anne that the call-up paper wasn't for their father at all, but for her. Anne began to cry. She couldn't believe the Germans would transport a girl of 16 all by herself.

The plan becomes a reality

When Otto Frank returned home at 5.00 p.m, after visiting a friend, he discovered what had happened. During the afternoon Edith Frank had gone out and brought back Otto's business partner, Herman van Pels. The van Pels family – Herman, Auguste and their son Peter – would go into hiding with the Franks. Otto and Herman discussed final plans and then Herman left to fetch their friend Miep Gies.

Miep came and took away clothing, returning at 11.00 p.m. that night with her husband Jan to take more of the family's possessions to a secret hiding place. The next day, a warm wet Monday morning, Anne was woken up by her mother at 5.00 a.m. The whole family dressed in several layers of clothing. It would have been too suspicious for a Jewish family to be seen walking in the streets carrying suitcases so they wore whatever they could. Miep arrived to fetch Margot and they cycled off to their secret destination.

At 7.30 a.m. Anne and her parents left Merwedeplein forever. Anne was upset about leaving their cat Moortje behind, but they all wanted to reach a place of safety and at that moment nothing else mattered as much. As they trudged the five kilometres north through the rain to Prinsengracht, Anne was told the whole plan for going into hiding. She had not known that their refuge was to be inside her father's workplace or that so much thought and energy had gone into creating their sanctuary. The original plan was to go into hiding on 16 July, but the date had been brought forward because of Margot's sudden call-up.

The hiding place revealed

Miep Gies was waiting for the Franks when they arrived at 263 Prinsengracht. She led them along the corridor on the first floor and up the wooden stairs to the second floor where Margot was waiting. The annexe was at the back of the building on the top two floors. A small narrow hallway containing a steep flight of stairs and two doorways led to the first three rooms. The door to the right led to the bathroom – a windowless room with a basin and small lavatory cubicle. A door from this room gave access to the sisters' bedroom. The other door in the hall opened into the Frank family's living room and Otto and Edith's bedroom, with a communicating door into Anne and Margot's bedroom. The hall staircase led to the two rooms the van Pels family would occupy. The first was a large room containing a gas cooker and a sink, which was to be Mr and Mrs van Pels' bedroom as well as a living room, dining room and study for all the occupants. The second, a tiny side room, would serve as a bedroom for Peter van Pels. Above these two rooms, reached by a steep staircase in Peter's room was an attic, a quiet place where Anne would later go to write in her diary. A few weeks after their arrival Victor Kugler thought the entrance to their hiding place should be disguised. He asked Mr Voskuijl, Bep's father, to make a heavy, hinged bookcase that would swing open like a door.

Anne's annexe

In her diary Anne confided: "The annexe is an ideal place to hide in. It may be damp and lopsided, but there's probably not a more comfortable hiding place in all of Amsterdam. No, not in all of Holland." It took a lot of hard work to make the rooms habitable, but after a couple of days of cleaning and scrubbing some sort of order was established. Bep Voskuijl and Miep Gies went shopping with the Franks' ration coupons so that the family would have something to eat. Otto Frank had thought to bring Anne's postcard and film star collection to the annexe – he had even brought a pot of glue and a brush! Anne happily plastered the walls of her room with pictures and soon it looked more like home.

Edith and Margot were deeply affected by the move to the annexe and it took them a couple of days to recover from the experience. Anne and her father threw

▲ *A false bookcase concealed the staircase to the annexe, as revealed here by Otto's friend Johannes Kleiman.*

themselves into making black-out curtains for the apartment. Later, Anne wrote: "These works of art were tacked to the windows where they'll stay until we come out of hiding." Black-out curtains were essential to block out light and to protect against prying eyes.

Deportation of Dutch Jews started in the summer of 1942, during night raids. Jewish people were rounded up by police and transported in cattle trucks to

▲ Tale of hatred: this wartime poster urges the
Langemarck Division of Hitler's SS to rid mainland
Europe of Jews before moving on to Great Britain.

Westerbork transit camp and from there to concentration camps in Poland (Auschwitz, Birkenau and Sobibor) and later to camps at Bergen-Belsen and Theresienstadt in Germany. Many tried to get exemption stamps in their ID papers or to obtain passports from other countries, but few were successful. Most escape routes were closed.

In the early years of the German occupation of Holland, the Dutch Resistance was not very effective. Religious and political differences hampered their organization. By 1942, however, they were helping to create false identity cards, find "hosts" who would take in Jews, and destroy registration offices where statistics helpful to the Nazis were kept.

By late 1944 about a quarter of a million non-Jewish Dutch were in hiding, while another 900,000 had left their homes to evade deportation to Germany as forced labour. Of the 24,000 Jews in hiding during the war, 16,000 survived, while 8,000 were discovered and then killed.

A typical teenager

Anne was a typically volatile young girl, and in the confined atmosphere of the Secret Annexe her feelings were sometimes exaggerated, even confused.

Anne felt that her mother got on better with Margot than with her, which was true to some extent as Edith Frank and Margot were much more in sympathy with one another. Margot was a quiet and studious 16-year-old, who was more of a companion to their mother. Anne wrote: "They're so sentimental together, but I'd rather be sentimental on my own." Anne adored her father, who was fondly nicknamed "Pim" by his daughters. She felt that he was the only one who really understood her. She often felt aggrieved, though, when Pim sided with Edith and Margot over some argument with Anne. She also hated the way in which her mother talked about her to people she described as "outsiders" (for example, Mr and Mrs van Pels). In reality, Anne's mother probably found the situation – being confined with a difficult teenage daughter – very wearing and needed someone to talk to about it. For her part Anne was spirited and independent-minded, often clashing with her mother in the way that many teenage girls do.

A teenager in hiding

After one particularly heated argument, over a book Margot was reading and she wanted, Anne let rip in her diary about her feelings for her mother and sister. She wrote that she loved them, but only because they were mother and Margot, and she didn't give a "dash" for them as people. She went on to say that she clung to her father because of the contempt that she felt for her mother. Towards the end of this diary entry, full of normal teenage self-righteousness, Anne says, "The worst part is that father and mother don't realize their own inadequacies and how much I blame them for letting me down. Are there any parents who can make their children completely happy?"

▶ A plan of the Secret Annexe at 263 Prinsengracht, where the Franks, van Pels and Fritz Pfeffer lived in hiding for more than two years.

Mr and Mrs van Pels' room

Rear attic window

Peter van Pels' room

Margot, Edith and Otto Frank's room

Anne and Fritz Pfeffer's room

False bookcase hides entrance to annexe

Shared lavatory

Stairs up

Anne's rebelliousness was no doubt fuelled by the frustration of her virtual imprisonment in the annexe and the fact that she felt the loss of her friends keenly. In the absence of friends, school and freedom, her imaginary friend Kitty became the outlet for her emotions.

The van Pels arrive

The van Pels (called the van Daans in Anne's diary) joined the Frank family in hiding on 13 July 1942. They should have arrived on the 14th, but from 13-16 July the Germans had been issuing mass call-up notices, so Mr and Mrs van Pels had decided to err on the side of caution and go into hiding as soon as possible. Anne's life became more interesting after the van Pels family moved in. It had been too quiet for her before, with no other focus but her immediate family; this had made her nervous and prone to bouts of tears. Peter van Pels was the first of the family to arrive at the annexe as the Franks were having breakfast. Anne's first impression of him was that he was a shy, awkward 16-year-old boy "whose company won't amount to much". Herman and Auguste

Auguste (left) and Herman van Pels, who shared the annexe with the Franks.

van Pels arrived half an hour later. Part of Mrs van Pels' luggage was a hatbox containing a large chamber pot. This greatly amused Anne and her parents.

While the Franks found the van Pels amusing in small ways, in her diary Anne said of them, "some people seem to take special delight not only in raising their own children but in helping others to raise theirs". Now Anne felt that she was being scolded by four adults, two of whom were not even her own parents. Most of the time her mother and father would spring to her defence over some criticism – usually levelled by Mrs van Pels – and Anne later confessed that without her parents' support she wouldn't have been able to cope so well with these scoldings. When a squabble developed over Anne's eating habits during one mealtime, Otto Frank retorted, "look who's calling the kettle black!". This silenced Auguste van Pels, who wouldn't eat beans or cabbage for dinner because she said they gave her wind. Anne was amused when Mrs van Pels blushed with embarrassment, as she so easily did.

From the start the two families ate their meals together and after three days Anne said it felt as if the seven of them had become one big family. Mr van Pels filled them in on what had happened when they'd left their flat. Edith Frank had left a note with a Maastricht address on it so that neighbours, friends and anyone else who enquired would think that they had gone there en route to Belgium and Switzerland. Mr van Pels reported that he had heard from several people that this was where the Franks had gone, so the trick had worked.

Room for one more

Tragic reports of what was happening to the Jews were getting more frequent by the day. Their friends in the office, who kept them informed, knew of a Dutch Jew who needed to find a "safe house" and they asked the Franks and van Pels if they would consider harbouring one more fugitive. The two families agreed that eight could eat as well as seven and there was just enough room for another person in their hiding place. So Miep's dentist, a man named Fritz Pfeffer, was the last person to join them. Otto also knew Pfeffer and was keen to help him.

Fritz Pfeffer was a 53-year-old man who had been living with a Christian woman several years younger than himself. He

was reported to be good with children, quiet and refined. Miep conducted the negotiations and tried to get him to come to the hiding place at Prinsengracht as soon as possible. Although Pfeffer could not come immediately, he was relieved to have found a hiding place and turned up at the annexe several days later.

The arrival of Fritz Pfeffer signalled a reorganization of the annexe. He was to share Anne's bedroom, while Margot moved in with her parents. At first, Anne thought Mr Pfeffer was a nice man, who was agreeable to sharing a room with her. She wasn't delighted at having someone she didn't know using her things, but she was prepared to make sacrifices for a good cause. With the impatience of youth, she was surprised that Pfeffer was so slow to catch on to the way in which things were done in the annexe. She wrote, "he asks everything twice and still can't remember what you've told him".

Anne soon revised her opinion of Mr Pfeffer as he turned out to be "an old-fashioned disciplinarian and preacher of unbearably long sermons on manners".

▶ *Fritz Pfeffer was a middle-aged dentist, who was unused to sharing his space with strangers, least of all a lively teenage girl.*

She felt that he made a bad situation worse by criticizing her in the same way as the others, and he reported her apparent faults and misdeeds to her mother. Anne was getting more and more fed up with everyone criticizing and complaining about her and she confided to her diary on more than one occasion about the unfairness of the situation.

Too close for comfort

Life in the annexe was hard on all the occupants. They lived in cramped conditions with almost no privacy, no fresh air and a daily eight-hour ban on talking. After a while each person's little ways and habits became extremely annoying to the others and disputes over "territory" became more frequent.

By 22 December 1942 Anne wrote that she was always being scolded for making too much noise. Everyone kept saying "shh" to her, and Mr Pfeffer had taken to "shhing" her in the night, when she so much as coughed or turned over!

Anne found one of Pfeffer's habits particularly aggravating. This was his Sunday morning exercise session at the crack of dawn. He would "lumber" about in the little room they shared, bumping into chairs as he dressed and making it impossible for her to sleep. In her diary entry of 28 November 1942 Anne complained about sharing "my far too narrow room with His Excellency …" She may have been a typical teenager, but these were exceptional circumstances.

Not surprisingly, Anne was disturbed by nightmares at this time, probably brought on by Pfeffer's tales of what was happening on the streets of Amsterdam.

Happy Hanukkah!

In December 1942 Hanukkah (the Jewish festival of light) and St Nicholas' Day almost coincided. For Hanukkah, candles were lit in the annexe and gifts exchanged, as was the custom. According to Anne, St Nicholas' Day was more fun, with surprise gifts for everyone, including their "protectors" downstairs.

The following year Anne hatched a plan with her father to cheer everyone up. At a quarter to eight in the evening they brought in a basket, which had been decorated with paper cutouts and bows. On top was a poem: "Let's not forget it's St Nicholas' Day, though we've nothing left to give away". The basket contained a shoe belonging to each person, with a small gift tucked inside. This gesture was typical of Anne's often warm-hearted nature.

Razias (night raids) by the Gestapo on Jewish homes were becoming more frequent and while the hideaways tried not to dwell on these events during the day, at night it was sometimes impossible to stop thinking about them. Sometimes Anne awoke in the middle of the night and cried out, disturbing the others and needing comfort and reassurance before she could go back to sleep. On these occasions, it was usually Anne's father who went to her, even though her mother was willing to do so and was always protective of her two daughters.

▼ *A view of the room in the Secret Annexe that Anne shared with Fritz Pfeffer, as it is today.*

Daily life in the annexe

For Anne, one of the worst aspects of living in the annexe was the effort of staying quiet throughout the day. No one could suspect that they occupied a part of the Prinsengracht business premises and therefore silence was essential during business hours.

It must have been very hard for the eight people waiting with bated breath. They dared not exercise, wash or flush the toilet during the working part of the day, although they could read, write, study and play games. From Monday to Friday the office hours at Trading Company Gies and Co were 8.30 a.m. to 5.30 p.m. with an hour or so for lunch. During this break the residents of the annexe gathered to eat, listen to the BBC's 1.00 p.m. radio broadcast and do any washing or cleaning that was necessary before they resumed their rule of silence until the end of the working day. In early August 1943 Anne documented their daily activities in detail in her diary. She made light of these daily events, but in reality life in the annexe

was not fun. Right from the start the occupants of the annexe made themselves useful. They pitted fruit for preserves, filled packets with gravy powder and did simple office work to relieve those downstairs of some of their workload. They also had to store and prepare their own food, which was obtained using black market ration books, paid for with the two families' savings. They bought 140 kg of beans and stored them in the attic.

One of the sacks burst while it was being carried up the stairs, sending a shower of beans cascading down on Anne. Mr van Pels showed a talent for making

▶ *Food was in desperately short supply in Amsterdam during the war years. This picture shows people queuing outside a shop.*

sausage and produced bratwurst and mettwurst sausages from the meat they bought on the black market. He made the sausages and strung them on a pole suspended from the ceiling. Everyone laughed at the sight of the curing sausages as they dangled comically overhead.

Human habits

"The strangest things happen when you're in hiding," Anne would write on 29 September 1942, regarding the bathing habits of the members of the two families. All they had to wash in was a galvanized tin tub and each person chose a different place in the building to wash. When it was their turn to have a bath they would take the tub to their preferred spot and carry out their ablutions in the privacy of their chosen surroundings. Everyone had a specific time to use the washing facilities, although less rigid rules applied to the use of the lavatory. With a touch of characteristic humour, Anne recounted Fritz Pfeffer's toilet routine and the urgent needs of the people kept waiting by him. She wrote, "He never

◀ *Anne spent much time looking out of the small attic window of the Secret Annexe, shown in this side view of 263 Prinsengracht.*

deviates or lets himself be swayed by the voices outside the door, begging him to open up before a disaster occurs."

While they had to remain in hiding, they didn't neglect their studies or reading. Mr Kleiman brought books to the annexe every week and always picked out two especially for Anne: "written for girls my age". Their friends in the office also organized a correspondence course in shorthand for those who were interested, and English, French and Dutch were taught by occupants of the annexe who had become reasonably fluent in these languages. Anne continued with her schoolwork too, and was progressing well with her Dutch. Every day, between the hours of 2.30–4.00 p.m., she used the table in her own (and Fritz Pfeffer's) bedroom for studying. She asked Pfeffer if she could extend her use of the table until 5.30 two afternoons a week. When he refused, Anne called in her father as mediator and Pfeffer reluctantly gave in. But in the way of many such petty squabbles, Pfeffer reacted by not speaking to Anne for two days.

To keep fit all the inhabitants of the annexe took part in an evening session of calisthenics – a form of exercise that could be done in a small space, and which promoted suppleness and muscular strength. Sometimes the inhabitants of the annexe would sing or even dance, but only after 6.00 p.m., when the workers had gone home, and then only very softly. In her diary, Anne made a note of her favourite hobbies. Top of the list was writing, including made-up stories, then genealogy (she spent hours researching the family trees of European royal families), next came history and mythology and last but not least pictures of film stars and family, many of which were found in her papers. The group also played games, which they had brought with them to pass the time. Sometimes they told jokes and riddles and reviewed books they had read.

Anne also discovered the dubious joys of voyeurism – she used a pair of binoculars at night to stare into the lit windows opposite. She commented: "I never knew that neighbours could be so interesting. Ours are, at any rate. I've come across a few at dinner, one family making a cine film and the dentist opposite working on a frightened old lady."

A radio lifeline

Apart from their helpers, the only contact they had with the outside world was through their radio. In Otto Frank's old office there was a large Philips wireless. They would all gather around this in the evenings when the office staff had gone home and experience a sort of freedom granted by

the airwaves. The annexe rules were that they could only listen to the radio

after 6.00 p.m., and not to German broadcasts (especially German news bulletins) unless they were classical

▶ *Anne decorated the wall of her room with pictures of movie stars and celebrities.*

KOM OOK
IN DEN GERMAANSCHEN
LANDDIENST
IN HET OOSTEN

.11

music programmes. By June 1943 the German authorities demanded that all private radios must be handed over. This was because the messages people were receiving indicated that the Germans were starting to lose the war. All over Holland people were trying to get hold of old radios, which they could hand in to the authorities in place of their own "morale boosters". Jo Kleiman had hidden a small radio set in his house and gave this to the members of the annexe when the office radio had to be handed in at the end of July.

An appointment with the annexe dentist

An old-fashioned foot-driven dentist's drill was found for Fritz Pfeffer. His first patient at the annexe practice was Mrs van Pels, who had two teeth that needed attention. When he started to scrape out the cavity in one of her teeth, he struck a nerve, making her jump out of the chair with the probe still embedded in the tooth. Eventually, with Anne and Mr van Pels holding her down in the chair, Mr Pfeffer finished the job. Anne was not impressed. "The whole scene resembled one of those engravings from the Middle Ages entitled 'A Quack at Work'."

◀ This poster urges Dutch people to collaborate with the Nazis by joining the "Landdienst", a labour service, to work on farms in the east and help the Nazi war effort.

Constant fear

Even at night their troubles could not be easily forgotten. Air raids and anti-aircraft gunfire often woke them from whatever rest they could get. Anne and Mrs van Pels were particularly affected by the noises. Anne would crawl into her father's bed, shaking with nerves, only to return to her own bed when the "all clear" sounded. On a particularly bad day the RAF made three raids on Amsterdam. As the bombs rained down, the Prinsengracht house shook and Anne clung tightly to her "escape bag", which contained all the things she would need if she and her family were forced to evacuate their hiding place in a hurry.

Heroic helpers

The majority of the Dutch population resented the German occupation of their country, although at first few did anything to oppose Nazi rule. Many people felt there was no middle ground and they had to make a choice between Fascism and Communism.

Most Dutch people's religious principles, coupled with their country's history, would not allow them to opt for a godless political system such as Communism. However, by the autumn of 1942 the German setbacks in Russia and North Africa and the end of Mussolini's regime in Italy encouraged those who wished to resist the Nazis.

Although some Dutch collaborators helped the Germans, they experienced passive as well as active resistance from many other Dutch citizens. The biggest contributor to the German war effort in the Netherlands was the NSB, the Dutch National Socialist (Nazi) organization. On an individual level, profit rather than political belief often supplied the motive for collaboration. Recruits from the Dutch male population were sought to fight on the German "Eastern Front" in Russia. In 1940–41 30,000 men and boys volunteered, and in April 1941 17,000 entered service with the Waffen SS, the military arm of the SS. Many others worked in supporting roles, helping to supply the troops, build roads or military installations, or act as police or guards in prisoner of war and concentration camps.

In 1943 vital records regarding population statistics were destroyed when Amsterdam's registration office was set on fire by a Resistance group. Files of records from other towns' registration offices also disappeared and were hidden away so that the Germans could not make use of the information they contained. Anne wrote in her diary about the Amsterdam fire, "One good piece of news is that the Labour Exchange was set on fire in an act of sabotage. A few days later the Register

▶ *Anton Mussert was the leader of the Dutch Nazi movement. Here he meets Hitler's hated and feared deputy, Heinrich Himmler (left), on 26 May 1942.*

◀ Miep Gies and Bep Voskuijl in 1945.

Office also went up in flames. Men posing as German police bound and gagged the guards and managed to destroy some important documents."

No place to hide

Thousands of Jews tried to hide from their German persecutors, but very few succeeded. The most important factor in the success or failure of dropping out of sight was obtaining reliable help. But finding somebody who was willing to help was only the first obstacle to be overcome. Sometimes the Resistance would find a "host" who would shelter a fugitive. However, the fugitive was taking an enormous risk, as their "host" would have no personal feelings of loyalty to sustain them over a long and stressful period of time.

Some Jews found themselves exploited by their hosts, who in effect blackmailed them (for jewellery and money) and then sometimes went on to denounce them to the authorities. The Franks and their fellow hideaways were very fortunate in their four helpers. These good people were Otto's office staff, whom he had known and trusted for many years. He

had even signed over his businesses to two of them (Kleiman and Kugler) for the duration of the war. He was especially friendly with Miep Gies and her husband Jan (a member of the Dutch Resistance), but each one of the helpers was encouraged by their own beliefs and sense of justice to help their friends, which is how they regarded the hideaways.

Anne wrote about their "protectors", the heroic people who helped them, but she only saw "the tip of the iceberg". There are many peripheral characters in her diary, such as the grocer who delivered the potatoes to the office every lunchtime. She didn't know that he was also involved with a Resistance group, and that he and his wife gave refuge to two Jewish men in their apartment until they were betrayed in 1944.

Obtaining food

In Otto's memoir he mentions the role of each of the "helpers". The two women, Miep and Bep, provided the food for all eight of the inhabitants of the annexe. Jo Kleiman and Miep's husband, Jan Gies, obtained black market (illegal because they violated the restrictions on goods) ration cards for the residents and also arranged the sale of jewellery when their money ran low. Mr Kleiman had a friend who ran a bakery chain in Amsterdam. He arranged to have bread delivered twice a week to the office, part of the cost of which was paid on delivery of the bread. The balance was to be charged to account and paid for when the war was over. Obtaining food and supplies was not an easy task. Many hours were spent queuing for groceries with no guarantee that any food would be left by the time the counter was reached. The rationing of butter and cooking fat was particularly severe and sometimes none at all could be obtained. Bep was also responsible for the supply of milk and fresh fruit to the annexe. Fruit was expensive and could only be obtained when prices were low. Since almost everything was bought on the black market, staying in hiding was expensive. Mies sometimes managed to get meat from a butcher friend of Mr van Pels, who had taken her to the shop before he went into hiding. To help out with the hideaways' finances, Victor Kugler sold spices without keeping traceable records. This money went towards the hideaways' provisions.

Keeping up the spirits

Apart from foodstuffs, clothes and medicines, the helpers also provided books, moral support and news from the outside world. Miep, Jan and Bep would occasionally stay the night in the annexe and this would raise everyone's spirits, giving some semblance of normality. At midday too, when the other workers had left the building, one or two of the helpers might have lunch in the annexe. Later, Miep remembered a night she spent there: "The quietness of the place was overwhelming. The fright of these people who were locked up here was so thick I could feel it pressing down on me. It was like a thread of terror pulled taut. It was so terrible it never let me close my eyes."

Carrying on "normally" became a

Breaking the law to shelter a Jew

It was an illegal act to shelter a Jew from the authorities; any helper had to be ready to face extreme and arbitrary punishment if caught. The penalties for defying the law could range from temporary imprisonment and torture to death in a concentration camp. These helpers were truly heroic souls, since nobody knew how long the war might last, or even if the Nazis would lose it.

calculated risk as everything a helper did had to be weighed up against the likelihood of discovery by another "law-abiding" citizen.

It was important that the helpers felt that they would be able to hold out against the odds and be successful in saving their friends' lives. The survival of those in hiding depended on them, which was a great and sometimes terrible responsibility. Miep, who felt morally bound to keep her friends safe, "never felt any desire to be free of the Frank family". She sensed their dependence keenly, with the exception of Anne who was nearly always bright and cheerful, greeting her friends with a barrage of questions and tales of life in the annexe.

A loyal network

Anne's helpers were lucky in one way in that they shared the burden with each other and most had the support of their own families. Miep had her husband Jan, Bep was helped by her father, Johan Voskuijl (who made the bookcase for the annexe), Jo Kleiman had the support of his wife; only Victor Kugler kept his involvement a secret.

By the autumn of 1944 things were

Miep Gies, a true friend

Born Hermine Santrouschitz in Vienna in 1909, Miep was sent to Holland in 1920 at the age of 11 as part of a programme for undernourished children. She grew up there, with foster parents, and never returned to Austria. She started working for Otto Frank in 1933. As Hitler rose to power in Germany and Nazism took hold, Miep, a Christian, became increasingly alarmed and appalled at the persecution of minority groups, especially Jews. She shared these views with Otto and often discussed politics with him. When Germany invaded Holland and the Frank family were put in immediate danger, Miep didn't hesitate to offer them help. In 1941 she married Jan Gies and became a Dutch citizen.

much worse for the Dutch population as a whole. German repression in Holland increased as the Nazis lost the initiative elsewhere in Europe and took out their frustration on the occupied Dutch. However, about 30,000 people were actively involved in resisting the Germans by listening to forbidden Allied radio broadcasts and distributing information through the then-established underground press.

At the beginning of the war no organizations existed in the Netherlands to help fugitives "go underground". For most Jews it was a question of finding Christian friends or acquaintances who were willing to help them, as with the Franks. It was unusual for a family to be able to hide together in one place. Often, children were brought to a sympathetic friend, who would take them in or find a "safe address" for them. Several thousand Jewish children were saved in this way, many finding homes with farmers in the countryside. Few saw their parents again. When a friend's grandchildren were brought to their house one night, Miep and Jan managed to find a student organization in Amsterdam that held a list of safe addresses where children could be brought. As the war went on, Jan became involved with the Dutch Resistance and, through his contacts, was able to obtain ration tickets, books and magazines for his friends in the Secret Annexe. When the Allies liberated Holland in April 1945, over 75 per cent of the Jewish population – more than 100,000 people – had been killed.

▶ *An unusual overhead view of a model of the room that Anne shared with Fritz Pfeffer, giving some idea of the crowded conditions in the Secret Annexe.*

Growing pains

On 12 February 1944, Anne wrote in her diary:
"I think spring is inside me. I feel it in my entire
body and soul . . . I only know that I'm longing
for something." With these words Anne summed
up her feelings of sexual awakening.

By the beginning of 1944, the
occupants of the annexe had been
in hiding for 18 months. Anne was
growing up quickly and while still quick-
tempered, she was becoming more
reflective and sympathetic. She and Peter
van Pels were opposites, but naturally
enough in the circumstances they became
attracted to each other. He was quiet and
self-conscious, and he admired Anne for
the way in which she expressed herself
and seemed never to be lost for words.
They were experiencing some of the same
frustrations – being cooped up and unable
to express themselves – and they found
that they could talk to each other about
their feelings. Peter's increasing
fascination with Anne seemed to come at
just the right time for her. She was lonely
and missing her friends and she
desperately needed to be appreciated. In

her diary, she wrote: "I sensed a strong
feeling of fellowship, which I only
remember having had with my
girlfriends." Soon Anne and Peter were
spending more and more time together.

Hopes for the future
As Anne and Peter talked – about all
sorts of things – their relationship began
to develop. Sometimes, they would sit in
the attic, looking at the sky, the trees and
birds and feel so close and so happy that
words were not necessary. At other times
they discussed the past, present and future
and what they might do when the war
was over. Peter wanted to find work on a
rubber plantation in the Dutch East

▶ *At 13 Anne was a vivacious, intelligent girl.
She never considered herself to be as beautiful or
clever as Margot, but those around her were aware
of her charm.*

70

Peter van Pels

Born on 8 November 1926 in Osnabruck, Peter had thick brown hair and blue eyes. Friends and relatives described him as shy and self-conscious, but with a sweet nature. In spite of Anne's initial, rather dismissive view of him, Peter's character often struck a chord with her. Like Anne, he loved the theatre and dressing up. On one occasion, to entertain their families, Peter put on one of his mother's very tight dresses and a hat, while Anne donned a suit and cap. "The grown-ups were doubled up with laughter." Anne also warmed to Peter because of his fondness for his cat Mouschi. Anne later described Peter as "honest and generous, modest and helpful."

Indies. He told Anne that he wouldn't want anyone to know that he was Jewish, a comment that disappointed her because she had such a strong sense of her identity. Anne had decided she would become a Dutch citizen and work as a journalist "and later on a famous writer". She was an avid reader and a good student. And as well as keeping up with her diary, she had started to write stories.

Still at odds with her mother, Anne felt

◀ *Peter van Pels was not talkative like Anne, but he was practical and good with his hands. He enjoyed carpentry and other chores.*

a common bond with Peter, whose own mother – she felt – was a shallow woman. Anne also sympathized with Peter because he was not at ease with himself ("Little does he know it's his awkwardness I find so touching.") and she knew that his parents often argued, which upset him. She started to write in her diary about love: "Love is understanding someone, caring for him, sharing his joys and sorrows. This eventually includes physical love."

Introspection and emotions

At this time, Anne had vivid dreams about her first "crush", Peter Schiff, whom she hardly knew. In real life the dream Peter and the real Peter merged into an ideal person whom Anne could love. As she began to examine her feelings for Peter van Pels, she became more analytical, and more critical, both of herself and those close to her. People had always told her that she was attractive, generous and funny, but now she wondered if she was over-confident and conceited, merely "a terrible flirt, coquettish and amusing". In one touching entry in her diary (7 March 1944) she wrote about how the changes in her life had affected her and how she had been struggling to come to terms with her own shortcomings. Anne also experienced some feelings of jealousy in relation to Peter. She was convinced that Margot harboured feelings for him as well and this made her unhappy. When Margot gave Anne a letter in which she explained that she was fond of Peter, but the fondness was that of a sister for a brother, Anne was relieved. She confided to her diary about her longing for a boyfriend, her love for Peter, and about beauty and happiness. "A person who's happy will make others happy; a person who has courage and faith will never die in misery!"

A red letter day

Anne's fondness for Peter mirrored – and to some extent replaced – her affection for her father. In one diary entry she wrote: "Peter's a terrific chap, just like father". On 15 April 1944 ("…a red letter day for me"), Peter kissed Anne for the first time, sparking off mutual feelings of excitement and pleasure. This may have been an adolescent love, but for these two young people, cut off from the world, it was their first and only experience of being in love. They found comfort in hugging and kissing and simply lying cradled in each other's arms. Anne told her diary: "Why should we wait until we've reached a suitable age? Why should we ask anybody's permission?"

Despite this defiance, Anne felt that she must, in all honesty, tell her parents about the growing relationship. Part of her probably wanted to share these exciting new feelings with someone too. In the end it was, of course, her father she decided to confide in. She found a quiet moment in which to tell him that she and Peter had become close and although they were just friends, their relationship could develop into something deeper. Otto was as understanding as he saw fit, but he warned his daughter not to get too intense – a danger when the two young people spent so much time in each other's company. He told Anne that she must be the responsible one because, although he liked Peter, he felt he was immature and easily influenced. Anne respected her father and listened to what he had to say, but she was very much a free spirit and she wouldn't stop going to the attic to be with Peter, as her father wished.

A growing independence

Soon after their conversation, Anne wrote her father a letter, in which she told him that she had fought hard to become an independent person, with no help from anyone, and now that she had succeeded she didn't need to account to her parents for her actions. The next day Anne and her father had a long talk, during which she realized how hurtful her letter had been to him. Full of remorse, she wrote later: "This is the worst thing I've ever done in my life. Anyone who deliberately causes such pain to someone they say they love is despicable, the lowest of the low." Anne was ashamed that she'd hurt her father. She determined to learn from this experience, be less self-righteous and more forgiving. With Peter's help, she felt she could develop a good character, be someone those she cared about would be proud of. "I'll take father as my example once again, and I will improve myself."

Even though things settled down after this, a couple of months later Anne confided to her diary: "No one understands me!" She and Peter continued to be close, but in Anne's view their relationship wasn't progressing and

Growing girls

Otto and Edith Frank kept a record of their two daughters' heights on the bedroom wall. The marks are still there today, at the Anne Frank house, and show that Anne grew more than 13 centimetres in two years. Before long, the clothes they had brought with them to the annexe became too small and had to be altered. Occasionally Miep would bring the girls a new item of clothing, but most of the time they had to make do. On 2 May 1943 Anne noted that her vests were "so small that they don't even come to my tummy".

she found this frustrating. She was impatient, wishing that Peter could be less reserved and more communicative.

Anne had changed from the schoolgirl who had first come to live in the annexe, lively and bright but often quarrelsome. She had been growing up in the most difficult circumstances and now spent more time thinking about all sorts of things, trying to make sense of the world she lived in. In one of the last entries in Anne's diary, she wrestles with the question that women were thought to be inferior to men and the injustice of this notion. At just 15 years of age, Anne was showing true depth of character and a wisdom beyond her years.

The outside world

During the two years that Anne and her family were in hiding, many events took place in the world that would end the war and shape the future of the rest of the twentieth century.

Anne was only aware of these events through radio broadcasts, news from the helpers and what little she could hear and see at night, peering round the edge of the black-out curtains that covered the office windows.

The "Final Solution"

In December, 1941 the Nazis, in their tyranny over the German nation, commenced *Endlösung*, the "Final Solution". This was a plan to carry out the systematic mass murder of European Jews. They based their plans on their previous partial extermination of disabled people in Germany in the late 1930s, in an attempt to "purify" the German race. On 20 January 1942 the Wannsee Conference was held near Berlin, chaired

▶ *As the Franks hid in Amsterdam, elsewhere the fate of thousands of European Jews was being decided. Here, Jewish people in Würzburg, Germany, are marched off to concentration camps.*

by Adolf Eichmann. This meeting put the finishing touches to the plan and "rubber stamped" the proposed deaths of 11 million Jewish people. Unknown numbers of "undesirable groups" were also to be killed in this purge, including political opponents, so called "anti-social elements", Jehovah's Witnesses, Russian prisoners of war and hundreds of thousands of gypsies.

Transportation of Jews

Miep told the occupants of the annexe about the mass round-ups of Jews during October 1942. She described the horrors of the transportation of people in cattle trucks to Westerbork, the large transit camp which many Jews had been through on their way into Holland from Germany. The Gestapo treated their Jewish prisoners with great cruelty, shaving their heads to distinguish them from Christians. Bep told them about the young men who were sent to Germany to work in the factories there. They also heard that the Germans would take hostages against any damage caused to buildings or transport useful to the

◀ *Suffering and despair is evident on the faces of this Jewish family in Warsaw, 1943.*

German military. Punishment for this offence was the execution of five innocent hostages if the Gestapo couldn't find the saboteurs responsible. Anne was appalled and wrote: "Fine specimens of humanity, those Germans and to think I'm actually one of them! No, that's not true, Hitler took away our nationality long ago."

News of the war elsewhere

The radio gave those in the annexe important news of what was happening outside Holland, in the theatre of war. In November 1942 they heard that the Russian city of Stalingrad had still not fallen to the Germans and that the British had started to win battles against the German army in North Africa. When they heard that the British had landed in Oran, Tunis, Algiers and Casablanca, and all but Tunis were in British hands, morale inside the annexe began to improve greatly.

When Fritz Pfeffer had joined them he told them what was happening to the Jews "on the streets". He described the green and grey army vehicles that drove up and down, taking away Jewish families. It was impossible to escape them, he said, unless you went into hiding. It seemed that the Germans already had lists of Jewish names, stating who lived where. Sometimes they would offer a bounty for each Jew captured. The round-ups usually happened at night and Jews captured in Amsterdam were taken and held in the Jewish Theatre before going on to Westerbork camp. From there they were usually transported to the infamous camps of Auschwitz-Birkenau and Sobibor in Poland.

The suffering of the Dutch

Sometimes Anne sat downstairs in the front office after dark and peeped through a gap between the heavy black-out curtains. From her vantage point she could see what went on in the streets. How she must have longed for a taste of freedom, just to be able to breathe fresh air and walk along the canal. She wrote about the neighbourhood in which they were hiding, about the dirty little children with runny noses who played outside. Later, she wrote in her diary that things were so bad in war-torn Holland that the children ran around in thin shirts and wooden clogs: "They have no coats, no socks, no caps and no one to

help them." Food and fuel were in short supply and many children were cold, miserable and hungry.

From her window Anne observed that people seemed to be in a tearing hurry. Bicycles whizzed past so quickly that she couldn't see who was on them. One evening she saw two Jews walking by. This sight was so unusual that she wrote, "I felt as though I were looking at one of the Seven Wonders of the World. It gave me such a funny feeling, as if I'd denounced them to the authorities and was now spying on their misfortune."

Anne also wrote about the tragedy of people who returned home to find their houses boarded up and their families gone. These Jews would have been taken away before making their long and possibly last journey to a concentration camp in Germany.

Allied bombers overhead

Almost every night Allied bombers roared overhead on their way to destroy the cities and industries of Germany. Apart from hearing the planes going over, the radio broadcasts also informed them

▶ *By 1943, Allied bombers were destroying German cities in huge raids. This is part of Hamburg.*

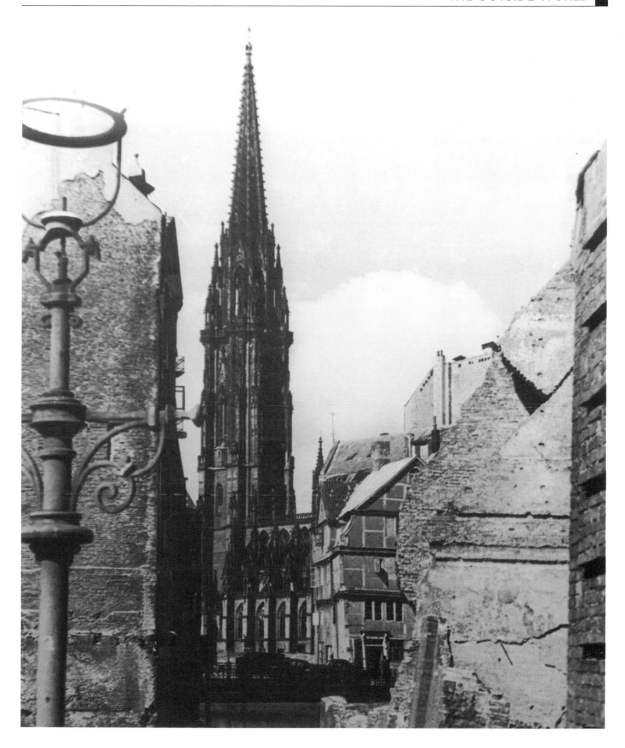

of the terrible damage and carnage on both sides. Thousands of tons of high explosive rained down night after night on the industrial centres and cities of western Germany, causing many casualties. Amsterdam was bombed several times and, on one memorable occasion, three times in one day.

On 19 July 1943 Anne wrote about one particularly damaging raid, which had taken place the day before, when North Amsterdam was targeted. Whole streets were destroyed and children were reported to be searching in the ruins for their parents. The initial death toll was 200 with many more people injured.

The fall of Mussolini

One of the best pieces of news that Anne and her family received was of the fall of Benito Mussolini, the fascist dictator of Italy. On 26 July 1943 Mussolini resigned and King Victor Emmanuel III of Italy took over the government of the country. By the beginning of August the Fascist Party had been banned and on 8 September the inhabitants of the Secret Annexe heard on their radio that Italy had unconditionally surrendered. The surrender had been agreed on

3 September, the day the British landed in Naples. In October the Allies broke through German defence lines and in November they seized Isernia, a key German position on the way to Rome. These advances gave everybody hope that the war would soon be over, even though the Germans still occupied northern Italy and would not be easily budged.

By February 1944 talk of the invasion of Europe by the Allies was in the air. There was speculation as to what would happen if the Allies landed in the Netherlands first. Would the Germans open the dykes to flood the country in order to defend it as they'd said they would? Anne noted on a map that large portions of Amsterdam would disappear under water, and the occupants of the annexe entertained themselves with suggestions of what they would do if this happened.

▶ *Benito Mussolini, the Italian dictator (on the left) with Adolf Hitler. Mussolini's downfall was welcomed by the inhabitants of the annexe.*

The final months

With every day that passed, the inhabitants of the annexe became more anxious. They continued to listen to radio broadcasts, following closely the progress of the Allies. Their friends in the office also kept them informed of the situation, at the same time endeavouring to keep their spirits up.

Anne and the others were worried about the increasing burden put on their helpers. On 26 May Anne's heartfelt entry in her diary revealed her state of mind: "One day we're laughing at the comical side of life in hiding, and the next day we're frightened, and the fear, tension and despair can be read on our faces … Let something happen soon, even an air raid. Nothing can be more crushing than this anxiety."

On 6 June 1944 – D-day – the Allies landed in Normandy, on the French coast, and were engaged in furious combat with German troops. The invasion of Europe was announced at 12 noon on that day in a BBC broadcast.

▶ *US troops wade ashore from a landing craft on D-day. The Allied invasion of Europe brought a sense of hope to the inhabitants of the Secret Annexe.*

84

"A huge commotion in the annexe!" Anne wrote in her diary. At last the hideaways could allow themselves to be cautiously optimistic about the liberation and an end to the war. Margot started to make plans to go back to school the following September.

Security slip-ups

In the months leading up to this, the hideaways had begun to relax their guard somewhat, almost without realizing it. They continued to go about their daily routine, observing the quiet times, but they were becoming more careless, perhaps forgetting not to flush the toilet during working hours or leaving belongings downstairs in the evening. On one occasion Mr van Pels left his briefcase and wallet in the office. When they were discovered the next day by one of the warehouse staff and shown to Kugler, he was forced to say that they were his. When Kugler returned van Pels' belongings, some money was missing from the wallet. All they could do was hope that whoever took it would be satisfied.

On 11 April 1944 the warehouse was broken into and, without thinking, Mr van Pels went down and shouted "police" to get rid of the burglars. A man and a woman shone a torch into the warehouse and Peter and Mr van Pels ran back upstairs as fast as they could. This incident shocked the occupants of the annexe more than any other. They were terrified that the burglars would alert the police and they would be discovered. So, for a day and two nights, over the Easter break, the hideaways hardly dared move. They sat whispering into the darkness and each time they heard a creak, someone would say "shh". They scrambled around, trying to find warm clothes and something to use as a toilet, but for the most part they stayed still. When they heard a rattling of the bookcase and saw a light right in front of it, they thought the end had come. But, as the increasingly tense hours went by, no more was heard. Like the others, Anne was terrified, but she showed great courage, comforting Mrs van Pels and trying to behave "like a soldier". Eventually, after they had risked phoning Mr Kleiman, Miep and Jan turned up and gradually everything returned to normal.

On another occasion Peter forgot to lock the outside door at night, something all the inhabitants of the annexe had been scrupulously careful about in the past. One evening he forgot to unbolt the door so that Kugler and the staff could enter in the morning. If it hadn't been for Kugler's quick thinking (he smashed one of the kitchen windows in the office), an employee would have climbed in one of the back windows! Much later, after the war, a man who had lived in one of the houses overlooking the back of 263 Prinsengracht as a boy, recalled that he and his friend had seen a girl at the window of one of the rooms at the back (the Secret Annexe). Later, when he saw a photograph of her, he realized this must have been Anne. He may have mentioned it to his parents in passing. At any rate, the hideaways were becoming less vigilant and several people probably knew or suspected they were there.

More security alerts

At the beginning of 1944 a succession of burglaries once again put fear into those hiding in the annexe. In February Mr van Pels disturbed an intruder when he went to do his evening rounds downstairs. He thought the burglar had run off into the night, but the following morning Peter found the front door open. It looked as if the intruder had let himself in with a key, hidden in the building while Mr van Pels was downstairs, probably watching him as he returned upstairs, and then let himself out. This was a very worrying development for the hideaways since it meant that someone almost certainly knew of their whereabouts and had a key to the building. From then on, they lived in fear, Anne noting in her diary: "Who can have our key? … If the thief is one of the warehousemen, then he now knows someone is in the house at night …"

Is the end in sight?

As the hot summer progressed, most of the talk in the annexe was of liberation. They hardly dared to hope, yet they couldn't stop themselves. At the same time those in hiding learned that there was a resurgence of anti-Semitism because many Dutch people believed that some captured Jews had denounced their protectors to the Nazis. With a remarkable degree of understanding for a girl of her age Anne wrote that people should be able to see the situation from both sides. She wondered how Christians would react if they or their families were being tortured. Would they eventually

give in? No doubt many would. "So why ask the impossible of the Jews?"

Anne celebrated her 15th birthday on 13 June and her gifts included "a lovely bunch of peonies from Peter". In July a glut of strawberries arrived in crates and "for two days there were nothing but strawberries, strawberries, strawberries …" This was followed by nine kilos of peas. On 21 July the inhabitants of the annexe heard of the assassination attempt on Hitler's life, this time by a general in the army. "Now at last things are really going well!" Anne told "Kitty".

Betrayal

Anne's last letter to her diary is dated Tuesday, 1 August 1944. Three days later, on the morning of Friday, 4 August, the German Security Service (SD) burst into the office at 263 Prinsengracht and told the workers to stay where they were. They marched into Kleiman's office and soon after, seeming to know what they were doing, went upstairs to the bookcase and opened the door to the Secret Annexe. They arrested everyone there,

◄ *By August 1944 Allied troops had fought their way inland. Here, British soldiers storm a German-occupied French farmhouse. Resistance was fierce.*

pausing only to let them collect a few belongings. When the Gestapo left with their prisoners, Bep, Miep and Jan went upstairs and rescued what they could.

The hideaways had almost certainly been betrayed, but it was never discovered by whom. The office staff had their suspicions – a warehouse worker called van Maaren had been stealing from the company and was said to have told a fellow worker "there are Jews hidden in the building", but he never confessed. One thing Kleiman and Kugler knew for certain was that some of the warehouse staff suspected or guessed there were people hiding at the back of the house. Van Maaren had even set traps, although when questioned by his employers he said this was to catch the burglar. No one could prove otherwise.

Aftermath

After their arrest, Anne and the other occupants of the Secret Annexe, along with Victor Kugler and Jo Kleiman, were taken to a holding cell in the Gestapo headquarters on Euterpestraata in South Amsterdam.

Miep Gies and Bep Voskuijl were allowed to remain at the office. It was thanks to Miep, who saved Anne's diaries, scattered papers and many of the family's photograph albums, that these precious belongings were preserved. When she went through the rooms of the annexe, after her friends had been taken away, she picked up what she could and without knowing why she took Anne's shawl from the back of the bathroom door. "Even though my arms were filled with papers, I reached out and grabbed the shawl with my fingers. I still don't know why." Later, Otto Frank gave the shawl to Miep to keep in memory of Anne.

◀ *Victor Kugler survived the war. He moved to Canada, where this photograph was taken in 1978.*

The arresting officer

Karl Silberbauer, an Austrian-born police officer, was in charge of the arrest of the people hiding in the Secret Annexe. He forced Victor Kugler to take him and his men upstairs and as they pulled back the secret door they drew their revolvers. Once inside, Silberbauer grabbed Otto's briefcase, scattering the contents (Anne's papers) all over the floor. The exposure of Silberbauer as the arresting officer was made by the Nazi-hunter Simon Wiesenthal in 1963. The newspapers quoted Silberbauer as saying that "the Frank family was just one of many Jewish families who were rounded up by the Gestapo".

Kugler and Kleiman were separated from the others and were taken away to another cell. Later, the man in charge of their arrest – Silberbauer – questioned the Franks, the van Pels and Pfeffer. He asked them if they knew of any other Jews in hiding in Amsterdam. When Otto said that he didn't, they were taken back to their cells for the night. The next day they were sent to a prison called the Huis van Bewaring on the Weteringschans. Here they were held for two days in dreadful conditions before being sent to Westerbork transit camp. Kugler and Kleiman were also interrogated, and later that evening they were taken to Amstelveensweg prison in Amsterdam. There they were questioned again about who owned the business on Prinsengracht and again Kugler insisted that he and Mr Kleiman owned the firm, not Otto Frank. This was the truth.

Westerbork

By this time, Westerbork transit camp had grown to be almost a town. It contained a hospital, a school, shops, a telephone exchange and even an old people's home. Beyond the fence was a farm, which was tended by the inmates of the camp. There was even a cabaret, a choir and a ballet troupe that gave performances. A railway line ran right into the middle of the camp. Every Tuesday morning trains would leave from here, taking large numbers of prisoners to the camps in the east.

Liberation begins too late

Brussels and Antwerp were liberated on 4 September 1944 and in the Netherlands a joyful hysteria was in the air. People thought that the liberation of their country was finally at hand. This became known as "Mad Tuesday" because the victorious Allied armies failed to show up and the occupying Germans became even more brutal in their desperation to hold on to their captured territory. Two days after this Kugler and Kleiman were taken from Amstelveensweg prison to Weteringschans, where the occupants of the annexe had been held on 6 and 7 August. On 11 September, they were sent to Amersfoort transit camp, where they did hard labour, punctuated by roll calls and beatings. Jo Kleiman suffered a gastric haemorrhage and was unable to continue working. On 18 September he was released due to illness.

Sent to almost certain death

The occupants of the annexe were transported from Westerbork to Auschwitz in Poland. They were on the last train to leave the Netherlands for the extermination camps on 3 September 1944. This deportation meant almost certain death for many who were crammed into the overcrowded cattle-cars. The last train from Westerbork contained 1,019 people. Each car was packed with about 75 people, who had only one small bucket of water for drinking and one larger one for use as a toilet. The journey to the camp took three days, during which time no one could stretch out because of lack of space. Many prisoners were already suffering from dysentery and some of the weakest died on the way.

When they arrived at their destination the prisoners were herded into groups of males and females. These groups were then divided into two columns: those who could work and those who could not. The group of non-workers included the sick, the elderly and children under fifteen. These people were told that transport was waiting to take them to the camp. Each lorry had a red cross painted on its side. Those who were too weak to walk scrambled aboard, only to be driven to immediate execution in the gas chambers inside the camp. Anne had just turned 15 and so escaped this fate.

The prisoners left behind endured an hour-long march to the gates of Auschwitz, over which were written the words "Arbeit Macht Frei" ("Work Brings Freedom"). A huge factory complex near Auschwitz, operated by the IG Farben

▶ *An exhausted female prisoner stares blankly through the barbed wire at Auschwitz.*

company, used large numbers of the camp inmates as forced labour. No thought was given to the safety of the workers, so the death toll in the factory was extremely high. Sick or well, people were forced to take risks to increase production. In truth, the only "freedom" from work was death.

Otto Frank survives

The fate of all but one of the inhabitants of the annexe was to die in a concentration camp in Poland, Germany or Austria. Only Otto Frank survived and it was he who recalled the death of Herman van Pels on 6 September, 1944 in the Auschwitz gas chambers just before they were dismantled in November 1944. It is not known in which concentration camp Auguste van Pels died, but this occurred sometime in the spring of 1945. She had been moved from Auschwitz to Bergen-Belsen, then to Buchenwald. The last recorded sighting of her was on yet another journey, this time to the concentration camp at Theresienstadt in Czechoslovakia on 9 April 1945 and it is likely that she died there. The van Pels' only son, Peter, died on 5 May 1945 in Mauthausen camp in Austria, having

been forced to march there, sick and hungry, from Auschwitz. It was just three days before the Mauthausen camp was liberated by the Allies. Fritz Pfeffer died in the Neuengamme concentration camp in Germany on 20 December 1944, after he had been transferred there from either Buchenwald or Sachsenhausen.

Fate of Anne and Margot

Otto, Edith, Margot and Anne Frank were in the Auschwitz-Birkenau camp together, but male and female prisoners were kept in separate sections of the camp. Edith succumbed to hunger and exhaustion and died on 6 January, 1945. At the end of October 1944, Margot and Anne were transported to Bergen-Belsen, near Hanover, Germany. Here a typhoid epidemic raged in the winter of 1944–45, the result of appallingly unhygienic conditions, which got worse as the camp's population swelled.

The disease killed thousands of prisoners, including Margot and, a little later, Anne. Anne died in late February or early March 1945, just weeks before

▶ *Conditions at Bergen-Belsen, where Anne and Margot died, were horrific. This photograph was taken shortly after the camp was liberated.*

Numbers of Jews killed, by country

Country	Number
• Germany	160,000
• Netherlands	106,000
• Czechoslovakia	277,000
• Hungary	305,000
• Poland	3,000,000
• Austria	65,000
• Romania	365,000
• France	83,000
• Lithuania	135,000
• Latvia	80,000
• Belgium	24,000
• USSR	1,000,000

British troops liberated the camp on 12 April 1945.

Jo Kleiman lived the rest of his life in Amsterdam, where he died in 1959. Victor Kugler managed to escape from his work group on 28 March 1945. He emigrated to Canada in 1955 and died in Toronto in 1981. Miep and Jan Gies stayed in Amsterdam and had a family. They stayed in touch with Otto Frank, who was reunited with them after the war. Bep Voskuijl died in Amsterdam in 1983 after a happy marriage and the children she had always wanted.

Otto Frank survived the camps. When Auschwitz was liberated by Russian troops on 27 January 1945, he was repatriated and returned to Holland via Odessa, a Russian port on the Black Sea, and Marseilles in the South of France. On 3 June 1945 Otto arrived back in Amsterdam and left no stone unturned in his quest to find out what had happened to his wife and daughters. He continued to live in the city until 1953 when he moved to Basel, in Switzerland, to be with his sister and family. That same year Otto remarried. His second wife was Elfriede (Fritzi) Markovits Geiringer, a Jewish woman who had also survived Auschwitz. Until his death in 1980, aged 91, Otto continued to share Anne's true story with the world.

◀ *British troops round up camp guards at Bergen-Belsen on the day of liberation, 12 April 1945.*

The diary:

A memorial to Anne

When Miep Gies picked up the scattered pages of Anne's diary and locked them in a drawer downstairs for safekeeping, it was an instinctive and protective action.

She couldn't have realized how important the diary would become, that millions of people would read the published version. Miep had not read Anne's diary, but she had no intention of letting the young girl's precious thoughts get into the wrong hands. She kept the diary, unread, hoping that one day she would be able to return it to Anne. After the war, she gave it to Otto, Anne's father, the only survivor of the Secret Annexe. Today, the diary can be seen in the Anne Frank Museum, which was established by Otto Frank at 263 Prinsengracht in Amsterdam.

A record for posterity

Although at first Anne had written the diary for herself, the chance hearing of a radio broadcast encouraged her to write a record for posterity. In 1944 she heard Gerrit Bolkestein of the Dutch government-in-exile on the radio. In his broadcast he said that after the war he would collect and publish eyewitness accounts of the Dutch people under the German occupation. This gave Anne, whose dream was to be a journalist, an added incentive for writing her diary. As well as acting as her confidante, it would be her first-hand account of a life in hiding during the occupation. In fact, she kept two versions: one was deeply personal; the other was written with a view to publication.

In Anne's memory

After the war Otto Frank decided to honour his daughter's memory – and grant her wish – by publishing the diary.

▶ *Otto Frank, a photograph taken before his death in 1980.*

◀ *The statue of Anne Frank which stands today in Amsterdam.*

The first edition, in 1947, was published in Dutch under the simple title *The Diary of a Young Girl*. The first print run was only a modest 1,500 copies. In his original edit, Otto selected passages from Anne's original unedited and amended versions. He took the decision to leave out several passages relating to Anne's sexuality, as well as some particularly hurtful comments she had made about her mother and others.

After Otto's death

When Otto died, at the age of 91, he left his daughter's papers to the Netherlands State Institute for War Documentation in Amsterdam. Since first publication, the authenticity of the diary had been in doubt (or at least thought by some to be a fake), so the Institute decided they must investigate and prove its authenticity once and for all. The *Critical Edition*, published in 1986, was the result of this investigation, which showed that the diary was the genuine article. In the *Critical Edition*, Anne's original unedited diary is referred to as "a", her second edited version is "b" and her father's

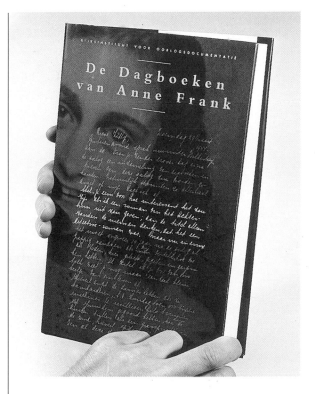

▲ *The* Critical Edition *of Anne's Diary, which was published in the Netherlands in Dutch.*

version (*The Diary of a Young Girl*) is "c". In the "b" version she used pseudonyms for most of the people mentioned, including herself. The van Pels were called the van Daans and Fritz Pfeffer was referred to as Albert Dussel. When Otto Frank came to edit the manuscript he respected Anne's wishes with regard to all but his family and helpers, who are referred to by their real names in the published versions.

A moving testament

Anne's diary is not only a testament to her lost youth but also the most poignant eyewitness account ever written of the Holocaust period. Anne's gift is in her words; through them she allows us to know her, her hopes and fears, and the secrets of her heart. Reading her diary, we experience with her the joys and setbacks of adolescence, the frustration and fear of a life in hiding, and the optimism that shines through in spite of everything: "If God lets me live, I'll go out into the world and work for mankind! I now know that courage and happiness are needed first!"

◀ *The* Critical Edition *was launched in Amsterdam in 1986. The publication of this edition of the diary was undertaken to silence once and for all people who thought that Anne's diary was faked. Here, the compilers explain their editorial methods – and the scientific examinations used – to the press.*

Glossary

Allegiance Loyalty to a government or monarch.

Annexe Extra, separate accommodation within a building.

Anti-Semitism Hostility towards Jews.

Arbitrary Decision made at random, usually by an oppressor.

Aryan Shared language of a group of people. A term improperly used in Nazi Germany to mean non-Jewish German.

Authentic Reliable, genuine.

Black market Place for illegally buying goods in short supply.

Blitzkrieg Aggressive military campaign intended to bring about quick victory.

Capitulate Surrender under certain conditions.

Collaborator Traitor who co-operates with the enemy.

Communism System of society in which everyone works for the common good.

Concentration camp Place where political prisoners or "enemy aliens" are detained.

Confidante Trusted person.

Constellation Group of fixed stars.

Counterpart Corresponding person or thing.

Decree Order or judgement decided by authority.

Democracy Government by the people, favouring social equality.

Denounce Inform against or publicly accuse someone.

Dyke Natural ditch or dam, especially those by the sea in Holland.

Edit Prepare for publication.

Elite Select group or class, considered to be the best.

Epidemic A widespread disease that affects a community at a particular time.

Expeditionary Fleet or men sent in for specific purpose, to do the job quickly.

Fascism Extreme right-wing or authoritarian views.

Fugitive Someone who is fleeing from danger.

Gas chamber A building used to kill prisoners by gas poisoning.

Genetically unfit Not of suitable origin, having "unsuitable" hereditary genes.

Gestapo Nazi secret police.

Great Depression The collapse of the world economy in 1929.

Holocaust Large-scale destruction, especially by fire.

Liberate Set free. The Liberation was the freeing of countries from German occupation during World War Two.

Memoir Personal account of events, written from memory.

Neutrality Exclusion from the hostilities of other countries; a neutral country is exempted from taking part in a war.

Paramilitary A military group that is organized in a similar way to the main military force, but is sub-ordinate to them (*from Greek para meaning "beside"*).

Paratroopers Parachute troops.

Posterity Future generations.

Prohibition An order that forbids something.

Propaganda Organized scheme to put forward political beliefs.

Pseudonym Made-up name.

Purge Elimination of people regarded as undesirable.

Qualm Uneasy feeling or doubt about a situation.

Ratify Formally accept or confirm agreement in writing.

Repatriate To return someone to the country in which they first lived.

Resistance Secret organization that resists foreign authority in a conquered country.

Resurgence Something that re-emerges or rises again.

Ruse Trick or device for deceiving the enemy.

Sabotage Deliberate destruction of enemy plans or equipment by covert (secret) means.

Sanctuary Place of refuge for fugitives from law.

Scapegoat Person getting the blame that should fall on others.

Segregate Separate or set apart.

Self-righteous Being right or virtuous in one's own eyes.

Skirmish Sudden outbreak of fighting.

Slump Sudden fall *(in prices)*.

Sterilization Depriving a living being of the power to reproduce by removing reproductive organs.

Succumb To give in to force.

Suppress Use force to restrain something.

Swastika Originally an ancient good luck symbol, depicting arms in a clockwise cross, it was used by the Nazis on their flag.

Synagogue Jewish place of worship.

Testament Written statement of beliefs.

Transit camp Place for the temporary accommodation of soldiers or refugees.

Underground press Publications produced in secret.

Timeline

1889 12 May Otto Frank is born in Frankfurt am Main, Germany.

1900 16 January Edith Holländer is born in Aachen, Germany.

1909 Otto returns to Germany from New York on the death of his father.

1914-1918 Frank brothers serve in German army during World War One.

1925 May 12 Otto and Edith marry.

1926 February 26 Margot Frank is born in Frankfurt am Main.

1929 12 June Anne Frank is born in Frankfurt am Main.

1931 March Frank family moves to 24 Ganhoferstrasse in the Poets' Corner of Frankfurt.

1933 January Hitler becomes Chancellor of Germany; **Summer** Otto makes plans to move to the Netherlands; **Autumn** Otto becomes manager of the Opekta-Works in Amsterdam; **5 December** Edith and Margot join Otto in Amsterdam.

1934 February Anne moves to Amsterdam and begins at the Montessori nursery.

1937 The van Pels leave Osnabruck, Germany and flee to the Netherlands.

1938 Fritz Pfeffer leaves Germany for the Netherlands; **9-10 November** Kristallnacht.

1939 Anne's maternal grandmother joins the family in Amsterdam.

1940 1 December the Opekta-Works moves to 263 Prinsengracht; **8 May** Otto transfers the ownership of his business to Victor Kugler and Johannes Kleiman, renaming it Trading Company Gies & Co.; **Summer** Margot and Anne attend the Jewish Lyceum in Amsterdam.

1942 January Granny Holländer dies; **12 June** Anne's 13th birthday; she is given the diary.

1942 5 July Margot gets "call-up" papers; **6 July** Frank family go into hiding in the Secret Annexe; **13 July** The van Pels arrive at the Secret Annexe; **16 November** Fritz Pfeffer moves in to share Anne's room.

1944 4 August The occupants of the Secret Annexe are discovered; **8 August** After being interrogated, those from the Secret Annexe are transported to Westerbork camp; **3 September** The prisoners are sent to Auschwitz concentration camp in Poland on the last train. A week after their arrival there, Herman van Pels dies; **October** Anne and Margot are sent to Bergen-Belsen; **20 December** Fritz Pfeffer dies in Neuengamme concentration camp.

1945 6 January Edith Frank dies in Auschwitz; **27 January** Otto Frank is freed when Auschwitz is liberated by the Russian Army; **March** Margot and Anne die of typhus in Bergen-Belsen, a few weeks before the camp is liberated by the British Army; **Spring** Auguste van Pels dies in Theresienstadt concentration camp; **5 May** Peter van Pels dies in Mauthausen concentration camp in Austria; **3 June** Otto Frank returns to Amsterdam.

1947 The diary of Anne Frank is published in Dutch.

1986 The *Critical Edition* of Anne's diary is published.

Further reading

Anne Frank House, (2001), *The World of Anne Frank*, London: Macmillan

Davidowitz, Lucy S, (1987), *The War Against the Jews*, London: Penguin

The Diary of Anne Frank, Critical Edition, (1989), New York and London: Doubleday/Viking

Frank, Otto H. and Pressler, Mirjam, translated by Susan Massotty, (1995), *Anne Frank: the Diary of a Young Girl*, New York: Doubleday; (1997), London: Penguin

Gies, Miep with Gold, Alison Leslie, (1987), *Anne Frank Remembered*, New York: Bantam Press

Gold, Alison Leslie, (1997), *Memories of Anne Frank: Reflections of a Childhood Friend*, New York: Scholastic Press

Lee, Carol Ann, (1999), *Roses from the Earth: the biography of Anne Frank*, London and New York: Viking Penguin

Lindwer, Willy, (1991), *The Last Seven Months of Anne Frank*, New York: Pantheon

Moore, Bob, (1997), *Victims and Survivors: The Nazi Persecution of the Jews in the Netherlands 1940-45*, New York: St Martin's Press

Muller, Melissa, (1999), *Anne Frank: the biography*, London: Bloomsbury

Tames, Richard, (1998), *Anne Frank*, Oxford: Heinemann

van der Rol, Rund and Verhoeven, Rian, (1993), *Anne Frank: Beyond the Diary*, New York and London: Penguin Group

Chronicle of the 20th Century, (1988), London: Chronicle Longman

Index